●●● Liz Driscoll

Common mistakes at

KET

... and how to avoid them

CAMBRIDGE
UNIVERSITY PRESS

CAMBRIDGE UNIVERSITY PRESS
Cambridge, New York, Melbourne, Madrid, Cape Town, Singapore, São Paulo

Cambridge University Press
The Edinburgh Building, Cambridge CB2 8RU, UK

www.cambridge.org
Information on this title: www.cambridge.org/9780521692489

First published 2007

Printed in the United Kingdom at the University Press, Cambridge

A catalogue record for this publication is available from the British Library

ISBN-978-0-521-69248-9 paperback

Produced by Kamae Design

Contents

When do I use full stops and when do I use commas?

1 Tick the correct sentence in each pair.

1 a I would like to sell a computer, it's two years old.
  b I would like to sell a computer. It's two years old.
2 a Cardiff, which is in Wales, is very interesting.
  b Cardiff which is in Wales is very interesting.

A sentence always begins with a capital letter and ends with a full stop (unless it is a question). All sentences have a subject (a person or thing doing the action): ***The plane*** *arrived at 10.30 pm.* ***It*** *was an hour late.* (*The plane, It* = subject)

We use a comma to show a short pause which separates parts of a sentence:
- in a list: *There's a bed, a wardrobe, a table and two chairs in my room.*
- in a procedure: *Go down this street, turn right at the junction and it's on the left.*
- before *for example, like* and *such as*: *There are many places to visit,* ***like*** *the lake.*
- before *but, so, then*: *I like my bike,* ***but*** *I'm selling it.*
- at the end of the first part of a sentence which begins with *if, when, after, before, while*: *If I see the book I want, I will buy it.*
- before extra information (and after it if there is no full stop): *I like my room,* ***which is nice and light.*** *My room,* ***which is nice and light,*** *is very small.*
- between a name and a description: *I want to buy* ***Face2Face, an English book.***
- before question tags: *You can look at your map,* ***OK?*** *It's nice weather,* ***isn't it?***

☆ A comma cannot separate two sentences.

2 Correct the mistake below.

> I've got a new computer. Because my old one was very slow.

loading

I've got a new .... one was very slow.

3 Add full stops and commas. Sometimes there are two sentences.

1 You must weigh the <u>rice,</u> wash it and soak it in <u>water.</u>
2 I want a pen friend in another country for example Australia
3 Before you leave England go and visit Oxford I love it
4 We saw *Syriana* a film by George Clooney
5 My flatmate who is from Russia is very nice
6 I've got a sister two brothers and a cousin I haven't got any pets
7 I'm going to buy a car so I don't need a bike
8 We waited ten minutes then we decided to walk

2 When must I use *I*?

1 Tick the correct sentence in each pair.

1 a You are coming here and am very happy.

 b You are coming here and I am very happy.

2 a I think will do my homework.

 b I think I will do my homework.

In general, we use subject pronouns (*I, you, he, she*, etc.) before verbs. This is because verb forms (*play/plays, played, have/has played*, etc.) refer to many different people (*I play / you play / we play / they play*, etc.). In addition, we always use *I* with *am*: **My friend and I enjoyed** the film. **She liked** the story and **I liked** the acting.

You don't need to use the subject pronoun in the second (and third) part of a sentence when the subject is the same as in the first part and the verb is in the same tense: **I got up** late, **had** a shower and then **went** out for breakfast.

We always use a pronoun after the verbs *hope* and *think*: *I **hope you** are OK. I **think I'll** sell my coat.*

We always use a pronoun after *because, but* and *so*: *I got up late **because I** was very tired.*

Remember to include the pronoun *it* at the beginning of sentences like these: *It's nearly six o'clock, so **it's** time to go. **It** was nice to see you again.*

2 Correct the mistake below.

I am tired, so decided to stay in bed all day.

I am tired, ... all day.

3 Rewrite the sentences using *I*.

1 am hoping to see you soon. ....*I am hoping to see you soon.*....................

2 think will go into town and buy a shirt. ....

3 bought the book, because liked the film. ....

4 my grandparents died and was very sad. ....

5 can play tennis, but don't play very well, ...

6 am tired today, so will sleep well tonight. ....

7 put the book on the shelf and left the library. ....

8 hope will see you soon. ....

When can I use an apostrophe before *s* ('*s*)?

1 **Tick the correct sentence in each pair.**

1 a I like this book. Its very useful.

  b I like this book. It's very useful.

2 a My sister's name is Maribel.

  b My sisters' name is Maribel.

We use '*s* as the short form of *is* and the short form of *has* in *has got/been*, etc. when we speak and when we write informally:

*I go to the market because **it's** very cheap.* (*it's* = *it is*)

*Brighton is interesting and **it's** got very good shops.* (*it's* = *it has*)

☆ Note that *its* (without an apostrophe) means 'belonging to it': *The lion ate **its** food.*

We don't use short forms at the end of sentences:

*'What time **is it**?'* *'**It's** four o'clock.'*

'Has your mum gone out?' *'Yes, **she has**.'* (not *'Yes, she's.'*)

We also use '*s* in *let's*:

*I'm hungry. **Let's** have something to eat.*

☆ Note that '*m* is the short form of *am*. Other short forms include '*re* (*are*), '*ve* (*have*), '*ll* (*will*), '*d* (*had* and *would*) and *n't* (*not*).

We also use '*s* to mean 'belonging to one person or animal'. We use *of* for things:

*I didn't go to my **cousin's** house last night.* (= the house of one cousin)

*Write your name at the top **of the page**.* (not *Write your name at the page's top.*)

☆ Note that *cousins' house* means 'the house of two or more cousins'.

2 Correct the mistake below.

You think it isn't cold, but it's.

You think it isn't cold, ...

3 **Rewrite the sentences with short forms where possible.**

1 The sea is very clear and it is great for swimming. The sea's ... it's great ....

2 What has that girl got in her hands? ....

3 You are not pleased with your marks, but we are. ....

4 I know! Let us go shopping and buy some clothes. ....

5 'What date is it today?' 'I think it is the eighth.' ....

6 The book has got a nice title, but I do not like its cover. ....

7 'Hello. Who is speaking?' 'It is Jane.' ....

8 The city is very nice and it has got lots of parks. ....

Test 1

1 Add the words in brackets to the sentences. Use commas where necessary.

1 I've got two sandwiches .... and a drink for lunch. (*an apple*)
2 I've got my keys .... ? (*haven't I*)
3 I like foreign food .... and pizza. (*such as pasta*)
4 After I left the nightclub .... (*I went home*)
5 My friend .... sits next to me. (*who is nice*)
6 Peel the carrots .... and then put them in the pan. (*chop them*)
7 My jacket's new .... (*so I wear it all the time*)
8 I'm selling my guitar .... and in good condition. (*which is two years old*)

2 Tick (✓) the correct sentence in each pair.

1 a I can write once a week. Is this OK for you? ....
   b I can write once a week, is this OK for you? ....
2 a Cambridge is an interesting place. Because it's got a university. ....
   b Cambridge is an interesting place because it's got a university. ....
3 a Let's meet near Piero's, the Italian restaurant. ....
   b Let's meet near Piero's the Italian restaurant. ....
4 a I get up at seven o'clock. It is dark. ....
   b I get up at seven o'clock, it is dark. ....
5 a Edinburgh is nice, but its very windy. ....
   b Edinburgh is nice, but it's very windy. ....
6 a I know someone who's got a guitar. ....
   b I know someone, who's got a guitar. ....
7 a I was there, but I didn't see my friends. ....
   b I was there. But I didn't see my friends. ....
8 a I like music. So I've got a lot of CDs. ....
   b I like music, so I've got a lot of CDs. ....

3 Rewrite the sentences using *I*, *it* or *we*. Use short forms where possible.

1 (is very hot today) ....

2 (are looking forward to your visit) ....

3 (maybe will meet our friends) ....

4 (don't want my bread, so you can have) ....

5 (like our new car because has got air conditioning) ....

6 (is dark, so need my torch) ....

7 (were at home last night) ....

8 (am buying because costs very little) ....

4 Write sentences. Use apostrophes (') where necessary.

1 itshalfpastthree ....
2 mybrothersjobisboring ....
3 icantrememberitsname ....
4 letshavelunch ....
5 itsatthebackofthebook ....
6 hiscarsgotfourdoors ....
7 werenothappyhere ....
8 thatsmyfriendspen ....

5 Are the sentences right or wrong? Correct those which are wrong.

1 Go and see the film. I'm sure you'll like. ....
2 I like my room It's quite big. ....
3 We went to the end of the street. ....
4 What date's it? ....
5 I've got my dads' watch. ....
6 I like fruit, for example grapes. ....
7 I do'nt like classical music. ....
8 I'm hungry. I think will have something to eat. ....

4 Do I need *a* in this sentence?

1 Tick the correct sentence in each pair.

1 a I went to party last night.
   b I went to a party last night.
2 a Oxford is a very old city.
   b Oxford is very old city.

We use *a* with singular countable nouns:
*I want to buy **a camera** for my mother.*

We use *an* before singular countable nouns beginning with the vowels *a, e, i* and *o*:
*I eat **an apple** every day.*

We also use *a* and *an* before an adjective + noun:
*Budapest is **a beautiful city**. It's **an interesting place**.*

We do not use *a* and *an* before an adjective if there isn't a noun:
Budapest is a beautiful city. It's an interesting place because it's old.

We use *an* before most nouns and adjectives that begin with *u* (*an umbrella / an uncle, an uncomfortable chair / an ugly building*). However, when a word begins with a /j/ sound, we use *a* and not *an*:
*We're studying **a unit** about 'a' and 'an'.*
*I don't wear **a uniform** at work.*
*A dishwasher is **a useful machine**.*

2 Correct the mistake below.

I'm staying in lovely hotel.

I'm staying .... hotel.

3 Rewrite the end of these sentences using the words in brackets. Use *a* or *an*.

1 Keanu Reeves is famous. (*actor*) ......*a famous actor*......
2 Spain is interesting. (*country*) ....
3 It was fantastic! (*match*) ....
4 London is expensive. (*city*) ....
5 My best friend is lazy. (*person*) ....
6 That's great! (*idea*) ....
7 I live in a block of flats. (*ugly*) ....
8 Who's good? (*student*) ....

5 A or *the*?

1 Tick the correct sentence in each pair.

1 a I like the living room in my house because it's very big.
   b I like a living room in my house because it's very big.
2 a I go to a dentist twice a year.
   b I go to the dentist twice a year.

We use *a*:
- after *there is*: *There's **a park** and **a swimming pool** near my house.*
- to mention a person or thing for the first time: *I've got **a friend** from Rome.*
- to describe what we do: *I'm **a student**. My dad's **a teacher**.*
- to describe ourselves: *I'm **a Chelsea supporter**. My brother's **a clever boy**.*

We use *the*:
- to mention a person or thing for the second time: *I walk through **the park** every day, but I don't go to **the swimming pool** very often.*
- when it is clear which person or thing we are talking about: *I like my class. **The teacher** is very good.*
- when there is only one person or thing: *I do my homework in **the living room**.*
- for places in a town (but not after *there is*): *the cinema / the theatre / the bank / the post office / the library / the station* (also *the airport*)
- for services: *the doctor / the dentist / the optician / the hairdresser*

2 Correct the mistake below.

I can see you
at a bus stop.

I can see you ....

3 Add *a* and *the* to these sentences.

1 I bought .....<u>a</u>..... cake and .....<u>a</u>..... banana, but I didn't eat ...<u>the</u>.... banana.
2 In my town, there's .... bank and .... cinema near .... station.
3 I know nothing about plants. I need to get .... book from .... library.
4 My uncle's .... doctor. He works in .... hospital in Canada.
5 Sydney is .... big city, but it isn't .... capital of Australia.
6 My brother's .... goalkeeper on his team. He's .... good footballer.
7 I work in .... shop in .... city centre.
8 I switched off .... light and closed .... door.

6 Do I need *the* in this sentence?

1 Tick the correct sentence in each pair.

1 a I work in an office in Milton Street.
  b I work in an office in the Milton Street.
2 a New York is the largest city in United States.
  b New York is the largest city in the United States.

We use *the*:
- with the names of cafés, hotels, restaurants, cinemas, theatres and museums:
  *I'll be at **the ABC café**. I went to **the Playhouse**. I like **the British Museum**.*
- with names which include *of*:
  *You can go to **the Bank of England** and **the Houses of Parliament**.*
- with some famous place names: *the White House, the Empire State Building, the Parthenon, the Vatican, the Kremlin, the Eiffel Tower, the London Eye*
- in *the United Kingdom* (*the UK*) and *the United States* (*the USA*)

We also use *the* with seas (*the Mediterranean Sea*), oceans (*the Pacific Ocean*), rivers (*the [River] Amazon*), islands (*the Bahamas*) and mountains (*the Andes*).

We use *the* with *north/south/east/west* for location. We don't use *the* for direction:
*Verona is in **the north** of Italy. It is **east** of Milan and **west** of Venice.*

We don't use *the* with street names or the names of stations, churches, airports, etc.:
***King's Cross Station** is in **Euston Road**. **Westminster Abbey** is in **Parliament Square**.*

2 Correct the mistake below.

My .... Odeon.

3 Add *the* to these sentences. Sometimes you need to add it twice.

1 I was in USA last week, but now I'm in Canada. ....the USA.........
2 Pedro works in Olympic Hotel near Oxford Street. ....
3 Sweden is in north of Europe, north of Denmark. ....
4 Have you been to Tower of London? ....
5 Natural History Museum is in west of London. ....
6 We went to Trafalgar Square and National Gallery. ....
7 Canary Islands are in Atlantic Ocean. ....
8 London Eye is next to River Thames. ....

1 Put the words in the correct order. Add *a* or *an* to each sentence.

1 I / TV / watched / film / on

....

2 grapes / have / and / I'll / some / orange

....

3 Milan / great / place / is

....

4 Spanish / Picasso / was / artist

....

5 got / has / university / Edinburgh

....

6 enormous / Brazil / country / is

....

7 I've / and / got / brothers / two / sister

....

8 unusual / is / name / Jania

....

2 Complete one sentence in each pair with *a* and the other with *the*.

1 a My cousin wants to be .... hairdresser when she leaves school.
   b I went to .... hairdresser on Monday.

2 a Excuse me. Is there .... post office near here?
   b I'll get some stamps at .... post office.

3 a .... student who writes the best story will win the prize.
   b .... student in my class was hurt in an accident last week.

4 a You'll find .... bathroom at the top of the stairs, on the right.
   b Each bedroom has .... bathroom with a jacuzzi.

5 a Who's .... man with red hair over there?
   b I saw .... man in the street with red hair.

6 a There's .... cinema in my town.
   b I go to .... cinema every week.

7 a There's someone at .... door. Can you open it?
   b There's .... door in the corner of the room into the kitchen.

8 a Do you know .... woman called Jill?
   b I know .... woman you're talking about.

3 Complete this description with *a/an* and *the*.

In my room there's (1) .... desk
and two chairs. I've got (2) ....
bookcase with three shelves. My
computer games are on (3) .... top
shelf. I play on (4) .... computer
every day. I've got (5) .... poster
of (6) .... Arsenal football team on
one wall. I'm (7) .... Arsenal
supporter, but I have never been to
(8) .... match.

4 Write sentences with *is* or *are*. Add *the* to these sentences. Sometimes you need to use it twice.

1 British Museum / in / Great Russell Street

....

2 Mexico / south of / United States

....

3 London Eye / near / Waterloo Station

....

4 Statue of Liberty / in / New York

....

5 Belfast / in / United Kingdom

....

6 Andes / in / west of South America

....

7 Dorchester / a famous hotel in / London

....

8 Canary Islands / in / Atlantic Ocean

....

5 Are the sentences right or wrong? Correct those which are wrong.

1 I'm reading the book about France. ....

2 The zoo in San Diego is very famous. ....

3 I bought two cakes, but I didn't eat smaller one. ....

4 My dad's good cook. ....

5 I visited the Acropolis in Athens. ....

6 This is awful place. ....

7 I've put your suitcase in a hall. ....

8 Oxford is on River Thames. ....

How do I talk about age?

1 Tick the correct sentence in each pair.

1   a   My mum has got forty years old.
    b   My mum is forty years old.
2   a   I want to sell my two years old bike.
    b   I want to sell my two-year-old bike.

We use the verb *be* to talk about age. We do not use the verb *have* or *have got*:
'How old **are** you?' 'I **am** twenty years old.' (not ~~I have twenty years old.~~)
My guitar **is** five years old. (not ~~My guitar **has got** five years old.~~)

When we talk about people and pets, we can miss out *years old*. With things, we always use *years old*:
'How old is your dog?' 'She's **six**.'
My favourite painting is nearly **five hundred years old**.

We don't always say *years old*:
'How old is your baby?' 'He's three **months old**.'
My sister's baby will be **one year old** in June.

We also use the singular form of *year*, *month* and *day* before a noun. We use hyphens before nouns:
I've got a **nine-year-old sister**.
We saw some **three-day-old lambs**.

2 Correct the mistake below.

My car is a mini and it is fifteen.

My car is a mini and ....

3 Underline the correct form.

1   This camera is <u>one year old</u> / one-year-old.
2   My CD player *is three year old* / *three years old*.
3   We've got a dog and a *ten-year-old* / *ten-years-old* cat.
4   My best friend *is eighteen years old* / *has eighteen years old*.
5   There are *two day old* / *two-day-old* baby birds in the nest.
6   My boyfriend will be *twenty-four years* / *twenty-four years old* next month.
7   This computer is only *nine months* / *nine months old*.
8   My grandparents *are eighty* / *have got eighty*.

15

How do I say the time and the date?

1 **Tick the correct sentence in each pair.**

1 a I start work at nine o-clock.

  b I start work at nine o'clock.

2 a My birthday is on the first of November.

  b My birthday is on the first November.

We use *it* (not *they*) when we ask and say the time. We use *o'clock* after a number when it is exactly that hour:

'*What time is it?*' '*It's two o'clock.*' (not '~~They're two o'clock.~~')

We don't use the 24-hour clock in spoken English. This is only for trains and planes. We use time expressions *in the morning/afternoon/evening* and *at night* to be clear:

*I will be with you at **eight o'clock in the morning**.*

*They arrived at **eleven o'clock at night**.* (not ~~twenty-three o'clock~~)

We can use the abbreviations *am* and *pm* in written English when we use figures:

*I will be with you at **8 am**. They arrived at **11 pm**.* (not ~~11 o'clock pm~~)

We can say times between the hours in two different ways:

It's twenty / half past eight. or *It's eight twenty / thirty.* (written as *8.20, 8.30*)

It's quarter / ten to nine. or *It's eight forty-five / fifty.* (written as *8.45, 8.50*)

We can say dates in two ways. We don't use *of* when we begin with the month:

We write: *July 22, 1995*   We say: '*July **the** twenty-second, nineteen ninety-five*'

            3 March 2006   '*the** third **of** March, two thousand and six*'

2 Correct the mistake below.

I woke up at .... yesterday.

I woke up at two o'clock pm yesterday.

3 **Rewrite these written times and dates in spoken English.**

1 11 am .... *eleven o'clock in the morning* ....

2 7 pm ....

3 September 4, 1839 ....

4 5.40 am ....

5 31 January 2010 ....

6 11 pm ....

7 August 16, 2002 ....

8 4.25 pm ....

When do I add *s* to verbs?

1 Tick the correct sentence in each pair.

1 a Juan works during the day and studies at night.
  b Juan works during the day and studys at night.
2 a My computer don't work very well.
  b My computer doesn't work very well.

We use the infinitive form of the verb with *I, we, you, they* in the present simple tense:
*My friends and I **like** football, so we **play** every day.*

We add -*s* to the infinitive form with *he, she* and *it*:
*Our teacher **likes** music and he **plays** the guitar.*

We have to make small changes to some verb endings:

-*es* after -*ss* / -*sh* / -*ch*:	*pass → passes, finish → finishes, watch → watches*
-*es* also:	*do → does, go → goes*
consonant + -*y* → -*ies*:	*try → tries, hurry → hurries, study → studies*
	also: *have → has*

We use the infinitive form in negative sentences:
*My brother doesn't **pass** his exams because he doesn't **study** very often.* (not ~~doesn't passes ... doesn't studies~~)

☆ Note that the verb *be* has three forms. We say *I am; we/you/they are*; and *he/she/it is*.
We make the negative with *not* and we often use contractions after pronouns:
*My sister **is** eighteen. She **isn't** very tall, but she's good at basketball.*

2 Correct the mistake below.

Tina's bike is very old. .... a new one.

3 Complete the sentences with the correct form of the verb.

1 My grandmother ......*watches*...... (*watch*) television in bed.
2 Our teacher .... (*not go*) home at lunchtime.
3 My parents .... (*come*) from the south of Spain.
4 A new bike .... (*cost*) 100 euros.
5 Nurses often .... (*work*) in hospitals.
6 My brother never .... (*tidy*) his bedroom.
7 Our flat .... (*not be*) very big.
8 My sister .... (*teach*) small children.

17

1 Rewrite the sentences so that they have the same meaning.

1 My brother is ten years old.
I've got a .... brother.

2 Our cat is thirteen.
We've got a .... cat.

3 My nephew is one year old.
I've got a .... nephew.

4 These chickens are two days old.
These are .... chickens.

5 My cousin is sixteen.
I've got a .... cousin.

6 My niece is three months old.
I've got a .... niece.

7 Our car is six years old.
We've got a .... car.

8 This painting is fifty years old.
This is a .... painting.

2 Look at the clocks and tick (✓) the correct time.

1  2  3  4

5  6  7  8

1 a It's ten o'clock at night. ....   b It's ten o'clock in the morning. ....
2 a It's twenty-five past three o'clock. ....   b It's twenty-five past three. ....
3 a It's quarter past six. ....   b It's half past six. ....
4 a It's twenty to four. ....   b It's twenty past four. ....
5 a It's five past eleven at night. ....   b It's five past eleven in the morning. ....
6 a It's ten to eight. ....   b It's fifty past seven. ....
7 a It's eight o'clock in the afternoon. ....   b It's eight o'clock in the evening. ....
8 a It's half past twelve. ....   b It's half past one. ....

3 Write the dates in spoken English.

1 The first man landed on the moon on July 20, 1969.

....

2 The first man swam from England to France on 24 August 1875.

....

3 Queen Elizabeth II was seventy-five on April 21, 2001.

....

4 The first men climbed Mount Everest on 29 May 1953.

....

5 Italy won the World Cup on July 9, 2006.

....

6 William Shakespeare died on 23 April 1616.

....

7 President Kennedy died on November 22, 1963.

....

8 The London Eye was opened on 31 December 1999.

....

4 Complete this text with the present simple form of the verbs.

This is John at his desk. He (1) ....
(*work*) in an office in the centre of the city. He
(2) .... (*not like*) his job very much.
John (3) .... (*finish*) work at half past
five and then he (4) .... (*go*) home.

John's friends (5) .... (*not see*)
him very often. Most evenings he
(6) .... (*stay*) at home and
(7) .... (*study*). He's got exams next
month. He (8) .... (*not want*) to stay
in the same job, so he must pass his exams!

5 Are the sentences right or wrong? Correct those which are wrong.

1 I must leave at five oclock. ....

2 My parents lives in a small flat. ....

3 Our teacher has got thirty years old. ....

4 My friend doesn't likes her room. ....

5 My sister has lunch with her friends. ....

6 The CD player is one years old. ....

7 I'll see you on ninth of January. ....

8 Carmen hurries home every day. ....

19

When do I add *ed* to verbs?

1 Tick the correct sentence in each pair.

1 a My parents called me last night, but I wasn't at home.

   b My parents call me last night, but I wasn't at home.

2 a I lost my friend's pen, so I gave him another one.

   b I lost my friend's pen, so I gived him another one.

We add *-ed* or *-d* to the infinitive form of the verb to make regular past simple forms: *I **enjoyed** the party on Saturday. I really **liked** the music.*

We have to make small changes to some verb endings:

consonant + *-y* → *-ied:*   *try → tri**ed**, hurry → hurr**ied**, study → stud**ied***

double the final consonant: *plan → plan**ned**, rob → rob**bed**, stop → stop**ped***

A lot of past simple verbs are irregular. Sometimes only one letter is different:

infinitive:	*come*	*drink*	*fall*	*get*	*give*	*know*	*lose*	*make*	*win*
past simple:	*came*	*drank*	*fell*	*got*	*gave*	*knew*	*lost*	*made*	*won*

Some verbs have the same infinitive and past simple form:

cost, cut, hurt, let, put, read (pronounced *red* in the past simple)

Other verbs have very different past simple forms:

infinitive:	*buy*	*do*	*feel*	*go*	*have*	*meet*	*see*	*sleep*	*speak*	*take*
past simple:	*bought*	*did*	*felt*	*went*	*had*	*met*	*saw*	*slept*	*spoke*	*took*

2 Correct the mistake below.

Do you like my hat?
I buyed it in Mexico.

Do you like my hat? .... it in Mexico.

3 Correct the mistakes in these sentences where necessary.

1 The walls were horrible, so I decorate them. ....*decorated*..........

2 This pen cost five dollars. ....

3 My brother studyed English when he was at school. ....

4 On Friday I met my friends and we go to a restaurant. ....

5 Two months ago I take my driving test. ....

6 I decided to stay at home this morning. ....

7 My brother come home at three o'clock this morning. ....

8 My parents buyed a washing machine yesterday. ....

20

I did or I have done?

1 Tick the correct sentence in each pair.

1 a We have played football yesterday.
   b We played football yesterday.

2 a I have finished my homework, so I can write to you now.
   b I finished my homework, so I can write to you now.

We use the past simple (*did*) when we say when something happened:
*I **watched** TV until six o'clock and then I **did** my homework.*
*I **bought** this camera two years ago. It **didn't cost** very much.*
*We **visited** a lot of museums when we **were** in New York.*

We use the present perfect (*have done*) when we don't say when something happened:
*I've **done** my homework. I can watch TV now.*
*I've **bought** a new camera. Here it is!*
*Julia isn't here. She's **gone** out.*

We use the present perfect to talk about our experiences:
*We've **been** to New York three times, but we've never **been** to Washington.*
*I **haven't seen** the film, but I've **read** the book.*

We make the present perfect with *have/has* + past participle (*done*). Note that a lot of past participles are irregular. Note also that *go* has two past participles. We use *gone* when someone hasn't come back; we use *been* when the person has come back.

2 Correct the mistake below.

> Paul isn't hungry, so he didn't eat his meal.

Paul isn't hungry, so he .... his meal.

3 Complete these sentences with the past simple or present perfect form of the verb.

1 I ....*left*............ (*leave*) school last year.
2 I .... (*read*) that book. I don't want to read it again.
3 I .... (*get up*) at half past seven this morning.
4 'What's the matter?' 'I .... (*hurt*) my leg.'
5 My parents .... (*not travel*) very much.
6 We .... (*not go*) to the theatre when we were in London.
7 I like George Clooney. I .... (*see*) all his films.
8 My sister .... (*start*) work in 2005.

21

12 For and since

1 Tick the correct sentence in each pair.

1 a The weather is nice since the weekend.
  b The weather has been nice since the weekend.
2 a This is my house. I have lived here for four years.
  b This is my house. I lived here for four years.

We often use *for* with the present perfect to talk about a situation that continues to the present. We use *for* to talk about the length of time:
Paula is in my class. I've known her for six months.
My mum works in a hospital. She has been a nurse for twenty years.

We also use *since* with the present perfect to say when the time period began. We do not use the present simple with *for* and *since*:
My parents have had a computer since 2004. (not My parents have a computer since)
I haven't seen Carlos since we were at primary school. (not I don't see Carlos since)

We use *for* and *since* with different time expressions. Here are some examples:
for   *an hour   three days   five weeks   six months   a long time*
since   *eight o'clock   last Tuesday   January   my birthday   I was ten*

We can also use *for* – but not *since* – with the past simple. We use *from* if we want to say when the time period began:
I studied maths for four years when I was at school. (but not I studied maths since)
We lived in Rome from 1999 to 2005.

2 Correct the mistake below.

Do you like this music?
I've had my guitar since three weeks.

Do you like this music? .... three weeks.

3 Correct the mistakes in these sentences where necessary.

1 We were married since July. ...*have been married*...
2 I've been a student since a long time. ....
3 Anna has knew her best friend since she was five. ....
4 I had my camera for four years and then I sold it. ....
5 I have a mobile phone since I was twelve and I use it a lot. ....
6 I haven't eaten for five hours. ....
7 Luigi has travelled a lot since he has left school. ....
8 We didn't play tennis since last month. ....

1 Complete this text with the past simple form of the verbs.

Paula (1) .... (plan) a surprise party for her sister's birthday last Thursday. She (2) .... (know) most of Jane's friends, so she (3) .... (try) to speak to them earlier in the week. She (4) .... (invite) them to come at half past seven on Thursday evening. Paula (5) .... (make) a cake and she (6) .... (put) candles on it. When Jane (7) .... (arrive) home at eight o'clock, she (8) .... (get) a big surprise. All her friends were waiting for her!

2 Complete the sentences with the present perfect form of the verbs.

1 A: What's New York like?
  B: I don't know. .... there. (*I / never / go*)

2 A: Where are your parents?
  B: I think .... to the cinema. (*they / go*)

3 A: Do you like the ABC café?
  B: Oh, yes. .... there lots of times. (*we / eat*)

4 A: Peter's quite tall now, isn't he?
  B: Yes, ... a lot. (*he / grow*)

5 A: Where's your homework, Barbara?
  B: Sorry, ... it at home. (*I / leave*)

6 A: Do you like Agatha Christie?
  B: Well, ... any of her books. (*I / not read*)

7 A: Why isn't Maria here?
  B: .... back home to get her glasses. (*she / go*)

8 A: Can you pay, Bruno?
  B: Sorry, ... my wallet. (*I / not bring*)

3 Underline the correct ending.

1 She went to London *on Saturday / since Saturday*.
2 My brother has seen that film *five times / five years ago*.
3 I stayed at my friend's house *since New Year's Day / until New Year's Day*.
4 I've had a headache *since last night / last night*.
5 I went to New Zealand *since three years ago / three years ago*.
6 I haven't seen James *for ten years / when I was at school*.
7 He studied physics *from 2003 to 2006 / since he went to university*.
8 My sister was a computer programmer *for three years / since 2003*.

4 Complete the sentences with the past simple or present perfect form of the verbs.

1 (*I / wait*) .... from half past two to three o'clock.
2 (*She / work*) .... in Cambridge for two years, but she works in London now.
3 (*They / not live*) .... with their parents since they were eighteen.
4 (*I / have*) .... this jacket for a month. Do you like it?
5 (*We / go*) .... home at eleven o'clock.
6 (*I / known*) .... Kate since 2001.
7 (*They / get*) .... married in February.
8 (*He / not be*) .... at work for three days. He isn't well.

5 Are the sentences right or wrong? Correct those which are wrong.

1 My dad's been a teacher since ten years.
   ....
2 My friend fall down the stairs yesterday.
   ....
3 Kate has been never to Rome.
   ....
4 My nails are long because I didn't cut them.
   ....
5 My new dictionary cost a lot of money.
   ....
6 We stoped at the shop to buy some bread.
   ....
7 My sister haven't been to London.
   ....
8 We have lived here for a long time.
   ....

When do I use *I am doing*?

1 Tick the correct sentence in each pair.

1 a   I buy a computer because I need one.
  b   I am buying a computer because I need one.

2 a   I'm getting a new camera for my birthday.
  b   I get a new camera for my birthday.

We use the present continuous for unfinished actions:
- to describe what is happening now
  *I **am doing** a grammar exercise at this moment.*
- with *today, this week*, etc.
  *He **isn't working** this week because he wants to paint his room.*
- to describe what is happening around this time
  *We're in London. We**'re having** a great time.*
- to talk about definite future plans
  *I am pleased you **are going** to Rome next week.*

Here are some examples of the present simple:
- *I **do** my homework every evening.* (regular habit)
- *I **work** in an office.* (permanent state)
- *We **go** to the doctor when we are ill.* (general truths)

We don't usually use the continuous form of *hope, know, like, love, need, want.*

2 Correct the mistake below.

This is my cousin.
He helps me to decorate my room.

This is my cousin. .... to decorate my room.

3 Underline the correct form.

1 *I'm meeting* / *I meet* my sister tomorrow morning.
2 *They're looking for* / *They look for* someone to rent a flat with them.
3 *I'm not having* / *I don't have* long hair.
4 Dear Michel, *I'm hoping* / *I hope* you're well.
5 *I'm selling* / *I sell* my car because it's too expensive.
6 Hi Jan, *I'm sending* / *I send* you this postcard from Paris.
7 I'm sorry *you're not coming* / *you don't come* here.
8 Please phone soon! *We're waiting for* / *We wait for* your call!

14 When do I use *I will*?

1 Tick the correct sentence in each pair.

1 a I see you next week.

  b I'll see you next week.

2 a I'd love to go with you, but I can't next week.

  b I'll love to go with you, but I can't next week.

We use *will* for things we decide now about the future:

* to make promises
  I'll be ready at two o'clock. (not ~~I'm ready at two o'clock.~~)
* to make offers
  If you like, I'll meet you at the station. (not ~~I meet you at the station.~~)
* after *think* and *hope*, and to make predictions
  I think you'll like my town. (not ~~I think you like my town.~~)
  It'll be nice to see you again. (not ~~It is nice to see you again.~~)

We use *shall I/we* only in offers:
Shall I close the window? (not ~~Will I close the window?~~)

We use *going to* for things we have already decided:
I'm going to stay at home this evening and write some emails. (not ~~I'll stay at home~~)

We use *would like/love/prefer* when we say what we want to do:
I'd like to go to the cinema tomorrow. (not ~~I'll like to go~~)

2 Correct the mistake below.

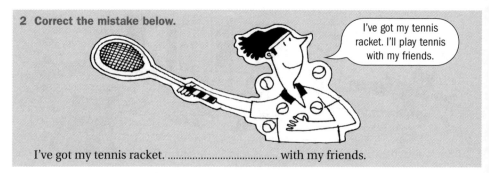

I've got my tennis racket. I'll play tennis with my friends.

I've got my tennis racket. .... with my friends.

3 Complete the sentences with the correct form of the verb.

1 ....*I'd love*............ (*I / love*) to go to New York with you.

2 We hope .... (*they / come*) and see us.

3 .... (*I / buy*) the bread, if you want.

4 'Let's meet at six.' 'OK then, ... (*I / see*) you at six.'

5 .... (*I / visit*) my friends at the weekend.

6 I am sure .... (*you / enjoy*) the film.

7 .... (*I / do*) the shopping for you?

8 I think .... (*it / be*) best if you come to my house.

How do I form questions?

1 Tick the correct sentence in each pair.

  1 a When you are arriving?
      b When are you arriving?
  2 a Did they play tennis last night?
      b Did they played tennis last night?

We change the position of the noun or pronoun with *am/is/are* (and *was/were*):
*The teacher **is** British. → **Is** the teacher British?*
*He**'s** going to watch TV. → **Is** he going to watch TV?*
*They **were** late for the exam. → **Were** they late for the exam?*

We also change the order of the noun or pronoun with these verbs:
- *will*: *It**'ll** be great. → **Will** it be great?*
- *have got/done*, etc.: *She**'s** done her homework. → **Has** she done her homework?*
- *can, could, must*, etc.: *They **can** swim. → **Can** they swim?*

We use *do/does* + infinitive with the present simple:
*The students **work** hard. → **Do** the students **work** hard?*
*The teacher **speaks** French. → **Does** the teacher **speak** French?*

We use *did* + infinitive with the past simple. Some verbs are irregular:
*She **went** home at eight o'clock. → What time **did** she **go** home?*
*I **did** my homework at school. → Where **did** you **do** your homework?*

2 Correct the mistake below.

    I don't understand the menu. .... English?

3 Write questions with *you*.

  1 I was tired. .... Were you tired? ....
  2 I watched TV last night. ....
  3 I'll be there. ....
  4 I want a drink. ....
  5 I could swim when I was three. ....
  6 I'm selling this dictionary. ....
  7 I've washed my hands. ....
  8 I had lunch at home. ....

Test 5

1 Complete the sentences with the present continuous or present simple form of the verbs.

1 My bike's got a flat tyre, so I .... to school this week. (*walk*)

2 Yolanda .... a shower. She's in her room. (*not have*)

3 My cousin .... on a farm. (*live*)

4 We .... on holiday to Thailand next month. (*go*)

5 I .... the answer to that question. (*not know*)

6 Rosa .... basketball two or three times a week. (*play*)

7 Pedro .... hard because he's got exams next week. (*work*)

8 I .... the weather is fine tomorrow. (*hope*)

2 Underline the correct form.

1 I hope *you'd like / you'll like* your present.

2 Your clock has stopped. *Shall I change / Will I change* the batteries?

3 *I won't forget / I don't forget* to wake you, I promise.

4 I'm meeting my friends at the cinema. *We're going to see / We'll see* a French film.

5 *I'll help / I'm going to help* you with your homework, if you like.

6 *We'd love / We'll love* to go shopping with you this afternoon.

7 I'm on holiday next week. *I'll stay / I'm going to stay* with my aunt.

8 I think *you enjoy / you'll enjoy* this book.

3 Write questions.

1 Paul has gone on holiday.

Where ....

2 She's bought some new clothes.

What ....

3 We were late for school.

Why ....

4 I saw Mark in the city centre.

When ....

5 Jane walked a long way.

How far ....

6 Be quiet! I'm watching TV.

What ....

7 I've got some money.

How much ....

8 They're going out later.

What time ....

4 In the box below, circle the correct words for each space, and complete the email.

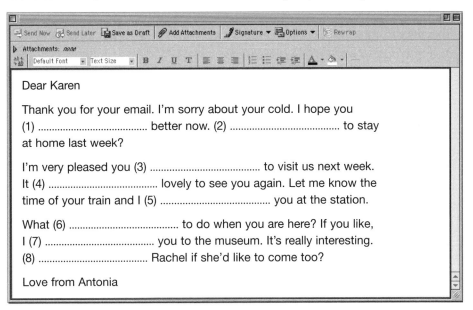

Dear Karen

Thank you for your email. I'm sorry about your cold. I hope you
(1) .... better now. (2) .... to stay
at home last week?

I'm very pleased you (3) .... to visit us next week.
It (4) .... lovely to see you again. Let me know the
time of your train and I (5) .... you at the station.

What (6) .... to do when you are here? If you like,
I (7) .... you to the museum. It's really interesting.
(8) .... Rachel if she'd like to come too?

Love from Antonia

1 're feeling	're going to feel	'll feel
2 Did you have	Do you have	You have
3 come	're coming	'll come
4 is	is being	will be
5 'll meet	'm going to meet	'm meeting
6 like you	will you like	would you like
7 'll take	'm taking	take
8 Do I ask	Shall I ask	Will I ask

5 Are the sentences right or wrong? Correct those which are wrong.

1 I'll go to the seaside tomorrow with my friends. ....

2 Does he work here? ....

3 I don't wear a hat at the moment. ....

4 Likes she her job? ....

5 I'm not going to go out this evening. ....

6 I think they come tomorrow. ....

7 What do you do now? ....

8 I'm in Greece. I have a wonderful holiday! ....

16 There and it/they

1 Tick the correct sentence in each pair.

1 a In London there are so many interesting places.

  b In London they are so many interesting places.

2 a You should visit Alicante because is great.

  b You should visit Alicante because it is great.

We use *there* to introduce new information. We always use a noun after *there*:

*In my room **there's a table** and **a chair**.* (not ~~In my room is a table and a chair.~~)

We use *it* for information that has already been mentioned. We can use an adjective or a noun after *it*:

*There's a cupboard too. **It's small** and **white**.*

*I like Cambridge. I think **it's** a lovely city.* (not ~~I think is a lovely city.~~)

We also use *it* to talk about times, dates, weather and distances:

*'What time **is it**?' '**It's** just after four.'*

*'**Is it** the twentieth today?' 'No, **it's** the twenty-first.'*

*The weather is horrible. **It's cold** and **it rains** all the time.*

*'How far **is it** to your house?' '**It's** ten kilometres.'* (not ~~There are ten kilometres.~~)

We also use *there* and *they* for plurals:

*'How many exercises **are there** in this book?' 'About eighty, I think.'*

*'**Are they** very difficult?' 'Not really.'*

2 Correct the mistake below.

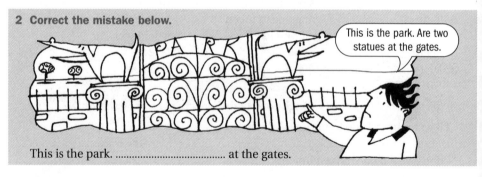

This is the park. Are two statues at the gates.

This is the park. .... at the gates.

3 Complete the sentences with *there's / there are* or *it's / they're*.

1 ....<ins>It's</ins>............... nearly eight o'clock.

2 If you like music, ... a concert tonight.

3 I quite like pears, but only when .... soft.

4 .... two boys from Moscow in my class.

5 The sun is shining and .... very hot.

6 I've got some new shoes, but .... not very comfortable.

7 I come here a lot because .... a nice place.

8 I went to Oxford, where .... a lot of old buildings.

Plural and uncountable nouns

1 Tick the correct sentence in each pair.

1 a There are sheeps in the fields.
   b There are sheep in the fields.
2 a Which countries have you been to?
   b Which countrys have you been to?

We add *-s* to singular nouns to make regular plurals: *piece → pieces, pound → pounds*

We have to make small changes to some plural noun endings:
-s, -sh, -ch, -x → + -es: *glass → glasses, dish → dishes, watch → watches, box → boxes*
consonant + -y → -ies: *country → countries, study → studies*
-f, -fe → -ves: *shelf → shelves, knife → knives, life → lives*

Some plural nouns are:
irregular: *man → men, child → children, person → people*
          one foot → two feet, a broken tooth → some broken teeth
the same as the singular noun: *one fish → six fish, a sheep → some sheep*

We can count plural nouns, but we cannot count *cheese, oil, sugar, water* or *money*,
for example. These are 'uncountable' nouns. We can say:
*I don't want **any cheese**.* or *I don't want **a piece of cheese**.*
*Can you lend me **some money**?* or *Can you lend me **three pounds**?*
☆ Note that *furniture, food, homework, information, music, time* are uncountable.

2 Correct the mistake below.

I am cooking some Italian foods this evening.

I am cooking .... this evening.

3 Complete the unfinished word.

1 Two chil*dren*.... were playing on the beach.
2 The man at the bar gave us two glas............. of water.
3 Is there any sug............. in this coffee?
4 I've got some new shel............. for my things.
5 What kind of furnit............. have you got in your room?
6 I couldn't walk any more. My f............. were hurting.
7 Phone this number for informat............. .
8 I got three English bo............. from the library.

When do I use *much* and *many*?

1 Tick the correct sentence in each pair.

1 a There's a lot of furniture in my room.
  b There's much furniture in my room.
2 a I'd like to visit as much places as you can show me.
  b I'd like to visit as many places as you can show me.

We use *much* with uncountable nouns:
- after negative verbs: *I didn't have* **much money**.
- in questions: **How much water** *do you need?*
- after *as/so/too*: *It takes* **too much time** *to walk to school*.

In the same way, we use *many* with countable nouns:
Are there many people *in the class?*
There are **so many museums** *in London. I haven't got time to visit them all.*

In general, we don't use *much/many* + noun after positive verbs. We use *a lot of* or *lots of* – especially in informal English:
There was **a lot of food** *at the party.* (not ~~There was **much food** at the party.~~)
You can find **lots of cinemas** *there.* (not ~~You can find **many cinemas** there.~~)

We can also use *a lot of* or *lots of* after negative verbs and in questions:
I didn't have **a lot of money**. or *I didn't have* **lots of money**.
Are there a lot of people *in the class?* or **Are there lots of people** *in the class?*

2 Correct the mistake below.

I want to watch TV, but I've got too many homework.

I want to watch TV, but I've got .... homework.

3 Underline the correct form. In some sentences both forms are correct.

1 I like _many_ / *much* kinds of music.
2 I want to sell *lots of* / *many* books.
3 Don't eat so *many* / *much* cheese.
4 I drink *a lot of* / *much* water every day.
5 Did you get *lots of* / *many* presents for your birthday?
6 Private lessons cost too *many* / *much* money.
7 We heard *a lot of* / *much* interesting music in Chile.
8 I didn't see *a lot of* / *many* films last month.

32

1 Add *there*, *it* or *they* to the sentences.

1 I sometimes go to the beach. Is near my town. ....

2 Are many students in your class? ....

3 I like your hair! I think is nice. ....

4 I've got a book. Are lots of photos in it. ....

5 I want some new shoes, but are expensive. ....

6 Is very hot here today. ....

7 Is a good film on TV tonight. ....

8 What date is today? ....

2 Look at the pictures. Write plural nouns.

1 **two b**............   2 **three f**............   3 **four p**............

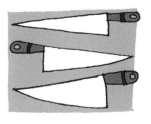 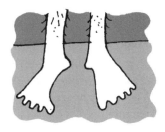

4 **three k**............   5 **two f**............

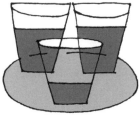 

6 **three g**............   7 **two b**............   8 **two w**............

3 Complete the text with *there's* or *there are*.

Greg is sitting at his desk, but he's not working. (1) .... some food on his desk and (2) .... some water in a glass. He's having lunch. (3) .... some shelves above the desk and (4) .... a radio on the bottom shelf. (5) .... some Russian music on the radio. Greg likes listening to the radio. He can see a field through the window. (6) .... some sheep in the field. (7) .... some children in the field too. They are playing football. Greg also wants to play football, but unfortunately (8) .... some homework in his bag. He has to do his homework before he can play football.

4 Underline the correct word in each sentence.

1 Are you going to need many *boxes / food*?
2 There were a lot of *furniture / men* in the room.
3 We haven't got much *hours / time*.
4 He's only ten months old. He hasn't got many *teeth / tooth*.
5 There are lots of *fish / salt* in the sea.
6 There wasn't much *information / people* at Tourist Information.
7 There's lots of *apples / fruit*. Help yourselves!
8 Is there a lot of *cheese / tomatoes* on your pizza?

5 Are the sentences right or wrong? Correct those which are wrong.

1 You can visit as many place as you like. ....
2 Too much people got on the bus. ....
3 Have you got a lots of friends? ....
4 Can you pass me the oil? ....
5 I've got a lot of homeworks this evening. ....
6 I'd like a piece of cake. ....
7 How many countrys are there in Europe? ....
8 I listen to much music. ....

Like, would like and want

1 Tick the correct sentence in each pair.

1 a I'd like to go swimming tomorrow morning.
  b I like to go swimming tomorrow morning.
2 a If you want the ticket, please phone me.
  b If you like the ticket, please phone me.

We use *like* to talk about things that please us:
* specific things: *I **like** your new glasses. Have you had them long?*
* general things: *I **like** going to the cinema, but I **don't like** fantasy films very much.*

We use *would like* to say what would please us either now or in the future. The negative *wouldn't like* only refers to now:
I'd like to go to the cinema this evening. (not ~~I like to go to the cinema this evening.~~)
*I'd like a good job, but I **wouldn't like** to work long hours.*

We can also use *want* instead of *would like*, but *want* is stronger and less polite:
*I **want** to go to the cinema this evening.* (not ~~I'll want to go~~ or ~~I'd want to go~~)
*I **don't want** to live in the country.*
*I was hungry. I **wanted** something to eat.* (not ~~I would liked something to eat.~~)

We also use *would like* and *want* when we make offers:
*'**Would you like** something to eat?'* (not ~~Do you like something to eat?~~)
*'**Do you want** something to eat?' 'No thanks. I've already eaten.'*

2 Correct the mistake below.

I've got a lot of homework. .... with you, but I can't.

3 Underline the correct form.

1 *I'd like* / *I like* some warmer gloves.
2 *We'd like* / *We'd want* to stay here until Monday.
3 *We didn't want* / *We wouldn't like* to stay out late last night.
4 I've got a computer, but *I don't like* / *I wouldn't like* using it for too long.
5 *They'd like* / *They like* to stay at home tomorrow.
6 *My friend wants* / *My friend will want* to visit me next week.
7 *I like* / *I would like* your new jumper. Where did you get it?
8 *Do you like* / *Do you want* a cup of coffee?

20 Do or to do?

1 Tick the correct sentence in each pair.

1 a I hope see you soon.
b I hope to see you soon.
2 a Do you recommend me stay in Barcelona?
b Do you recommend me to stay in Barcelona?

We use the infinitive (*do*) after *will, can, must, should* and their negative forms:
*I **can swim**, but I **can't swim** very far. We **can go swimming** at the weekend.*

We also use the infinitive (*do*) after the negatives *don't/doesn't* and *didn't*:
*I played football last night, but I **didn't play** very well.*

We use *to* + infinitive (*to do*) after:
* *want* and *would like* (see Unit 19), and *would love/hate/prefer*:
  I'd hate to live in another country. I'd prefer to stay here.
* the verbs *decide, expect, forget, hope, plan, promise, need*:
  *I **hope to get** a job one day, but I **don't need to think** about it yet.*

We use a noun/pronoun (usually a person) + *to* + infinitive (*to do*) after:
* *want, would like*, etc.: *I **want you to go** home now.* (not *I want that you go*)
* *expect, need, ask, tell, teach, recommend*: *I **don't need you to help** me.*
☆ Note that after *suggest*, we don't use *to*: *I **suggest you go** home.*

2 Correct the mistake below.

You shouldn't to work so hard. You're always tired.

You .... so hard. You're always tired.

3 Add *to* to these sentences where necessary.

1 I'd love .....to..... speak better English.
2 I won't .... tell her what you said.
3 What do you suggest we .... do?
4 I promise .... write when I get there.
5 You mustn't .... be late for the exam.
6 I asked him .... get me a present from Paris.
7 We didn't plan .... buy a new car.
8 I forgot .... do my homework last night.

36

When do I use *doing* after verbs?

1 Tick the correct sentence in each pair.

1 a We like play basketball.
  b We like playing basketball.
2 a I'm interested in buying a dictionary.
  b I'm interested to buy a dictionary.

We use the *-ing* form (*doing*) after these verbs:
- *enjoy, finish, stop*: *I **enjoy listening** to music.*
- *suggest* when the speaker is included in the suggestion:
  *I **suggest leaving** early.* (= I suggest we leave early.) (See also Unit 20.)

We also use the *-ing* form (*doing*) after an adjective + preposition:
*I'm interested **in learning** Chinese.* (not *I'm interested in learn Chinese.*)
*My friend is thinking **of having** a party.* (not *My friend is thinking to have a party.*)

We can use either the *-ing* form (*doing*) or *to* + infinitive with the verbs *like, love, hate, start, begin*:
*I **like texting** my friends.* or *I **like to text** my friends.* (not *I like text my friends.*)
*We **started doing** our homework at 6.30.* or *We **started to do** our homework at 6.30.*

We also say *go* + *-ing* with a lot of sports. Note that we don't use *go* + *-ing* to talk about ability or to say how far/well we are able to do something, etc.:
*We can **go sailing** on the lake.* (not *We can go sail on the lake.*)
*I **go swimming** every morning. I usually **swim** fifty lengths.*

2 Correct the mistake below.

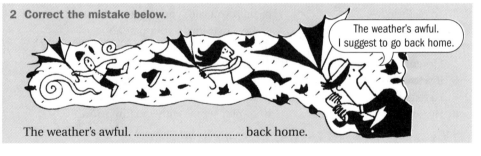

The weather's awful.
I suggest to go back home.

The weather's awful. .... back home.

3 Tick (✓) the sentences which are correct. In some pairs both sentences are correct.

1 a I'm interested in do judo. ....
   b I'm interested in doing judo. .....✓......
2 a Stop doing that! ....
   b Stop to do that! ....
3 a I hate getting up early. ....
   b I hate to get up early. ....
4 a Let's go skiing in January. ....
   b Let's ski in January. ....
5 a We love to watch TV. ....
   b We love watching TV. ....
6 a He started studying in May. ....
   b He started to study in May. ....
7 a I'm no good at to spell. ....
   b I'm no good at spelling. ....
8 a We can go skiing. ....
   b We can ski. ....

Test 7

1 Complete the questions with the words in brackets.

1 .... classical music? (*you / like*)

2 .... something to drink? (*you / want*)

3 .... a clean towel? (*you / would like*)

4 .... home? (*she / want / go*)

5 .... here? (*they / would like / stay*)

6 .... to restaurants? (*they / like / go*)

7 .... outside? (*he / would like / play*)

8 .... television? (*she / like / watch*)

2 Match the sentence endings with the beginnings.

1 You shouldn't	a to tell me what happened.
2 I'd really love	b help you with your homework.
3 He likes tennis, but he can't	c say anything to your parents.
4 I want you	d to pass his exams.
5 I forgot	e play very well.
6 If you want, I'll	f to have an accident in the car.
7 I'd really hate	g to clean my teeth this morning.
8 He hopes	h to play tennis with you tomorrow.

1 ☐   2 ☐   3 ☐   4 ☐   5 ☐   6 ☐   7 ☐   8 ☐

3 Underline the correct form. Sometimes both forms are correct.

1 Why don't we go *jogging / to jog* tomorrow morning?

2 I started *learning / to learn* English when I was five years old.

3 Is your friend any good at *run / running*?

4 Most people hate *getting / to get* up early.

5 I suggest *use / using* a dictionary.

6 I finished *doing / to do* my homework at midnight last night.

7 Are you thinking of *take / taking* an exam?

8 My dad started *learning / learn* English when he was 40.

4 In the box below, circle the correct words for each space, and complete the text.

I have decided (1) .... a sports club because I need (2) ....
some more exercise. I'm quite slim and I want (3) .... that way. I'm
interested in (4) .... squash lessons, so last night I went to a class. It was
hard work! The class started at half past seven and we finished (5) .... at
ten o'clock. I didn't (6) .... very well, but I enjoyed it. I hope
(7) .... a bit better next time! I suggest you (8) ....
squash – it's great!

1 join	joining	to join
2 get	getting	to get
3 stay	staying	to stay
4 have	having	to have
5 play	playing	to play
6 do	doing	to do
7 be	being	to be
8 try	trying	to try

5 Are the sentences right or wrong? Correct those which are wrong.

1 I like a new black jacket. ....

2 We asked them move the furniture. ....

3 We'd like emailing each other every day. ....

4 I expect to pass my driving test next time. ....

5 I'll want to see you soon. ....

6 You can to visit your favourite places. ....

7 Do you enjoy listening to music? ....

8 I'd prefer living in another country. ....

22 Other, others, another and each other

1 Tick the correct sentence in each pair.

1 a I will send you other postcards.

  b I will send you others postcards.

2 a Shall we meet us in front of the bus station?

  b Shall we meet each other in front of the bus station?

We use *another* (one word) + singular noun:

*I had **another** biscuit because they were so nice.* (= one more biscuit)

*I moved to **another** country.* (= a different country) (not ~~I moved to other country.~~)

We use *other*:

- + singular noun to refer to a second person or thing:

  *I've got two cousins. Henri lives with us, but my **other** cousin lives in the USA.*

- + plural noun when we mean 'more of the same kind':

  *I play football and I do lots of **other** sports.* (not ~~I do lots of others sports.~~)

We use *the/my other* as a noun when we refer to the second of two things or people and *the/my others* as a noun when we refer to the rest of a group. We can also say *the/my other one(s).* (See Unit 23 for *one* and *ones*.):

*I've got some new shoes. I'll throw **my others** away.* or *I'll throw **my other ones** away.*

We use *each other* when we say that A does the same thing to B as B does to A:

*Anna and I looked at **each other** and laughed.* (not ~~Anna and I looked at us~~)

2 Correct the mistake below.

I'm tired. I think I'll sleep for an other hour.

I'm tired. I think I'll sleep ....

3 Complete the sentences with *another, other, others* or *each other*.

1 I painted some of the pictures and my sister painted the ....*others*............ .

2 I like rock and lots of .... types of music.

3 I've known Mauro for ages, but we don't see .... very often.

4 I know .... people like modern art, but I don't.

5 I'm no good at basketball, but the .... on my team are fantastic.

6 I'm sorry, I'm busy. Can we go to the nightclub .... time?

7 One of my feet is longer than the ....

8 It was noisy where we lived, so we moved to .... flat.

One and ones

1 Tick the correct sentence in each pair.

1 a I don't need this ruler because I have a new one.
  b I don't need this ruler because I have a new.
2 a I'm not sure which hand she hurt, but it's the one she writes with.
  b I'm not sure which hand she hurt, but it's one she writes with.

We use *one* so that we don't repeat a singular person or thing:
*I couldn't find a shop assistant, but then I saw **one**.* (one = a shop assistant)

We use *ones* so that we don't repeat a plural person or thing:
*I've got some new glasses, but I prefer my old **ones**.* (not ~~my olds~~ or ~~my old~~)

We often say *this/that one* and *these/those ones*, and *the one(s)* and *which one(s)*:
*That shoe is OK, but **this one** has got a hole in it.*
*I'd like some grapes. Can I have **those ones** over there?*
*'Which bike is yours?' '**The one** by the wall.'* (not ~~The one bike~~)
*'I've lost my gloves.' '**Which ones**?'*

We can say either:
* *another* or *another one*: *I like those sweets. I think I'll have **another** (one).*
* *the/my other* or *the/my other one*: *You buy this CD and I'll buy **the other** (one).*
* *the/my others* or *the/my other ones*: *I'm wearing my new jeans. **My others** are at the cleaners.* or ***My other ones** are at the cleaners.*

2 Correct the mistake below.

I like both these hats.
I don't know which one
hat to buy.

I like both these hats. I don't know .... to buy.

3 Complete the questions with an adjective with the opposite meaning and *one/ones*.

1 Do you prefer a hard bed or ....*a soft one*............ ?
2 Is that a new bag or is it .... ?
3 Did you use the big envelopes or .... ?
4 Were they hard questions or .... ?
5 Did you carry the heavy suitcase or .... ?
6 Were you with the young women or .... ?
7 Would you like a fast car or .... ?
8 Are you wearing your long skirt or .... ?

Old, older, the oldest

1 Tick the correct sentence in each pair.

1 a It's the most cheap way to get here.
  b It's the cheapest way to get here.
2 a I like this room because it is biger than my old one.
  b I like this room because it is bigger than my old one.

We add *-er* to the adjective (*old*) to make the comparative (*older*) and *the + -est* to make the superlative (*the oldest*). For example: *cheap* → *cheaper* → *the cheapest*

We have to make small changes to some adjective endings:
consonant + *-y* → *-ier / -iest: easy* → *easier* → *the easiest*
double the final consonant: *big* → *bigger* → *the biggest*

We add *more* before long adjectives to make the comparative and *the most* to make the superlative: *interesting* → *more interesting* → *the most interesting*

Some comparatives and superlatives are irregular: *good* → *better* → *the best*
bad → *worse* → *the worst*   *far* → *further* → *the furthest*

We use *than* when we are comparing two people or things. When we are comparing more than two, we use *in* + singular (*in the class/world*, etc.) and *of* + plural (*of the seven sisters*, etc.). For periods of time, we use *of*:
*Thierry is **the tallest of** the players, but he's **the worst in** the team. He's **worse than** Robert. It was **the hottest** day **of** the year. I got up **later than** usual.*
☆ Note that adverbs such as *late* have comparative and superlative forms.

2 Correct the mistake below.

I am the taller person in the team.

I am .... in the team.

3 Complete the sentences with the comparative or superlative form of the adjectives.

1 I answered ....the easiest........... (*easy*) questions first.
2 It is .... (*hot*) in the afternoon than in the morning.
3 I like films, but I think books are .... (*interesting*).
4 .... (*good*) place to meet is the station.
5 It was .... (*happy*) day of my life.
6 Which are .... (*nice*) – the blue shoes or the brown ones?
7 My friend had .... (*expensive*) dish on the menu.
8 It's .... (*far*) to my house than you think.

42

Test 8

1 Tick (✓) the sentences which are correct. In some pairs both sentences are correct.

1 a My shoes are the ones with the leather straps. ....
   b My shoes are ones with the leather straps. ....

2 a The cakes were nice, so I had another one. ....
   b The cakes were nice, so I had another. ....

3 a I couldn't find a shirt I liked, and then I saw one on Saturday. ....
   b I couldn't find a shirt I liked, and then I saw one shirt on Saturday. ....

4 a These are my old sunglasses. I don't know where my others are. ....
   b These are my old sunglasses. I don't know where my other ones are. ....

5 a I've got one earring, but I don't know where the other one is. ....
   b I've got one earring, but I don't know where the other is. ....

6 a Most people liked his latest film, but I preferred the others. ....
   b Most people liked his latest film, but I preferred the others ones. ....

7 a My bicycle is too small, so I'm looking for a new one. ....
   b My bicycle is too small, so I'm looking for a new. ....

8 a I wanted a sandwich, but I wasn't sure which ones. ....
   b I wanted a sandwich, but I wasn't sure which one. ....

2 Write sentences with the comparative or superlative form of the adjectives. Remember to add *than, in* or *of*.

1 Paul is / tall / his brother

....

2 I think politics is / interesting / sport

....

3 Midday is / hot time / the day

....

4 Some players are / bad / me

....

5 My sister's baby is / happy / her three children

....

6 The London underground is / long / the world

....

7 He's / famous person / his town

....

8 I'm / good at chess / my sister

....

3 Is *other* correct in these sentences? Replace it with *another, others* or *each other* where necessary.

1 I can't meet you today. We'll have to meet other time. ....
2 Margrit and I have known other for a long time. ....
3 I like football and other sports. ....
4 I liked her first book, so I think I'll try other one. ....
5 Paul's here, but the other haven't arrived yet. ....
6 I've found one sock, but where's the other one? ....
7 My friends all live near other. ....
8 Two fingers were broken, but I didn't hurt the other. ....

4 In the box below, circle the correct words for each space, and complete the text.

My bike is really too old, so I have decided to buy (1) .... A friend came to the shop with me. There were lots of bikes to choose from. (2) .... I really liked was (3) .... in the shop, so I asked to see some (4) .... The shop assistant showed me a second-hand bike which was (5) .... My friend and I looked at (6) .... and laughed. This bike was in (7) .... condition than my (8) .... !

1 another one	other one	the other one
2 The one bike	The one	The ones
3 expensive	more expensive	the most expensive
4 other bike	other bikes	others bikes
5 cheaper	more cheap	more cheaper
6 another	each other	the other
7 badder	worse	worser
8 old	one	old one

5 Are the sentences right or wrong? Correct those which are wrong.

1 I don't need this bag because I bought an other. ....
2 This is best beach near here. ....
3 I like the green shoes, but not the reds. ....
4 It was the most boring film I've ever seen. ....
5 The longest river of the world is the Nile. ....
6 I needed a pen, so I bought one. ....
7 Trains are more faster than coaches. ....
8 Can I have other drink, please? ....

44

When do I use capital letters with people and places?

1 Tick the correct sentence in each pair.

1 a We stayed in a hotel near Heathrow Airport.
  b We stayed in a Hotel near Heathrow Airport.
2 a I live with my mum and dad.
  b I live with my Mum and Dad.

We use capital letters with:
- letter beginnings and endings: *Dear Wendy, ... Love from Yolanda*
- members of the family when used as names: *Hello, Mum / Uncle Paul*
- people's names and titles: *Mr Grey, Dr Smith, King Juan Carlos, the President*

We use small letters for family members and jobs, and for titles in a general sense:
*My **uncle** is my **mum's** brother. He's a **doctor**.*
*There has never been a female **president** of Italy.*

When names of places are in two parts, we use capital letters for both parts:
*We went to **Hyde Park** in the morning and then shopping in **Oxford Street**.*
*The (**River**) **Thames** flows into the **North Sea**.*

We do not use capital letters when we use these words in their general sense:
*I think **Lake Como** is the most beautiful **lake** in the world.*
*I live in **Walton Street**. It's a small **street** near the canal.*

2 Correct the mistake below.

I'd love to sail on the Nile, the longest River in the world.

I'd love to sail on .... in the world.

3 Rewrite these sentences using capital letters where necessary.

1 They live in a town near london. .... *They live in a town near London.* ....
2 The pacific ocean is the deepest ocean. ....
3 My new address is 761 beach avenue. ....
4 The sea is at the end of my road. ....
5 You can meet mr and mrs brown this evening. ....
6 The queen's youngest son is called prince edward. ....
7 My aunt's husband is an engineer. ....
8 The hotel is opposite richmond station. ....

26 How do I use *at* and *in* with places?

1 Tick the correct sentence in each pair.

1   a   I'll be at your house at half past three.
    b   I'll be in your house at half past three.
2   a   How long are you going to stay in Australia?
    b   How long are you going to stay at Australia?

We usually use *in* with places when we say where a person or thing is:
*I live **in** a town **in** the south of Italy. Our house is **in** a small street **in** the city centre.*

We also use *in* in the following expressions:
- *in bed, in hospital, in prison*
- *in the sky, in the world*
- *in a newspaper/book, in a photo/picture*

We use *at* with:
- events: *at a party, at a concert, at a football match*
- very precise locations: *at the door, at the bus stop*

We use *at* in the following expressions:
- *at home, at my friend's house, at work, at school, at university, at college*
- *at the airport, at the station*
- *at the doctor's, at the hairdresser's*
- *at the cinema, at the library*
- *at the top / at the bottom (of the page)*

2 Correct the mistake below.

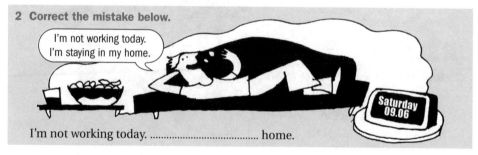

I'm not working today. .... home.

3 Complete the sentences with *at* or *in*.

1   I'll be back ...*in*.... London next week.
2   I have never been .... hospital.
3   My friend met me .... the coach station.
4   We went walking .... the mountains.
5   I saw the advert .... a magazine.
6   My cousin is studying .... London University.
7   I wrote my name .... the bottom of the letter.
8   My grandparents have a small house .... the country.

How do I use *by* and *in/on* with means of transport?

1 Tick the correct sentence in each pair.

1 a You can come here by your bike.
   b You can come here on your bike.
2 a We went to Sweden on ferry.
   b We went to Sweden by ferry.

We use *by* to say how we travel. We usually use *by* with *come, get, go, travel + to*:
*My friends want to go to Brighton **by car**, but I want to travel **by train**.*

We say *by bike / by car / by train / by underground / by bus / by coach / by ferry / by plane*. We also say *by air*. When people walk somewhere, we say that they *go on foot*.

We do not use *by* if we include *a/the* or *my/our*, etc. with the means of transport. We use *in* with *a/the/my/our car* (and *a/the taxi*), and *on* with the other means of transport:
*We'll go there **in my car**.*
*Travelling **on the underground** isn't cheap.* or *Travelling **by underground** isn't cheap.*
☆ Note that we don't use *to* before *here/there* and *home*.

You can also say *ride a bike* and *drive a car*.
*I **rode** my **bike** to London.* or *I went to London **by bike**.*
*My sister **drove** her boyfriend's **car** to Scotland.*

2 Correct the mistake below.

It's a nice day! I'm going to work by the foot.

It's a nice day! I'm going to work .... foot.

3 Tick (✓) the sentences which are correct. In some pairs both sentences are correct.

1 a Let's go home by bus. .....✓......   b Let's go home on the bus. .....✓.....
2 a We'll go there in the car. ....   b We'll go there on the car. ....
3 a Going by train is faster. ....   b Going on the train is faster. ....
4 a He went by air. ....   b He went by plane. ....
5 a How far is it in foot? ....   b How far is it on foot? ....
6 a We're driving to Edinburgh. ....   b We're going to Edinburgh by car. ....
7 a They went by boat. ....   b They went by the boat. ....
8 a I often drive my bike. ....   b I often ride my bike. ....

1 Complete the sentences in each pair with the same word. Use a capital letter for one of the words.

1 *hill*
   a They live in .... Road.
   b Let's walk up the ....

2 *ocean*
   a The Pacific is the largest .... in the world.
   b Hawaii is in the Pacific ....

3 *aunt*
   a My .... is going to visit me.
   b I sent .... Julia a postcard.

4 *canal*
   a The Panama .... was opened in 1920.
   b We're going on a boat on the .... next week.

5 *professor*
   a That's .... Brown, who works at the university.
   b She became a .... after 20 years at the university.

6 *street*
   a Is there a newsagent's in this .... ?
   b Broad .... is in the city centre.

7 *princess*
   a Who is .... Caroline?
   b A .... is a female member of a royal family.

8 *park*
   a I go jogging in the .... most mornings.
   b Central .... is in New York.

2 Underline the correct sentence ending.

1 There's someone in *the door / the kitchen.*
2 Kate's ill, so she's at *bed / home.*
3 The answers are at *the bottom of the page / another book.*
4 I met John when I was in *hospital / a party.*
5 Neil works at *Cambridge University / the middle of town.*
6 I saw a plane in *the sky / the airport.*
7 She's meeting me at *the cinema / Oxford Street.*
8 I read it at *a book / the hairdresser's.*

3 Complete the sentences with *by*, *in* or *on* where necessary. If no word is necessary, leave a space (–).

1 You can go to Heathrow Airport .... the underground.
2 I like travelling .... air. It's quicker than the train.
3 Do you ride .... your bike very much?
4 It's not too far, so maybe I'll go .... a taxi.
5 Going into town .... bike is better than using the car.
6 We went to Sicily .... the ferry.
7 I sometimes drive .... my parents' car.
8 London to Oxford .... the coach takes about two hours.

4 In the box below, circle the correct word for each space, and complete the text.

My sister lives (1) .... London, and I usually drive there. Last time, however, I decided to travel (2) .... train. What a mistake! I had to take a bus (3) .... the station. I waited half an hour (4) .... the bus stop, but no bus came. In the end, I went to the station (5) .... foot. I then waited half an hour (6) .... the station, and when a train came, there were no empty seats (7) .... it! I'll go (8) .... the car next time!

1	at	in	on		5	by	on	to
2	by	in	on		6	at	in	on
3	at	in	to		7	by	in	on
4	at	in	on		8	by	in	on

5 Are the sentences right or wrong? Correct those which are wrong.

1 I lost my gloves in a football match. ....
2 How many dogs are there in the picture? ....
3 George Washington was the first US President. ....
4 We went on holiday by the plane. ....
5 Lake Superior is the largest Lake in the world. ....
6 Mr and mrs Smith are our neighbours. ....
7 I came home by taxi. ....
8 dear Lola and Marcos, ...
   I hope you're well.

When do I use *at, in* and *on* with time expressions?

1 Tick the correct sentence in each pair.

1 a I'll visit you on Friday night.
  b I'll visit you at Friday night.
2 a Please call me in the evening.
  b Please call me at the evening.

We use *at* with:
- times: **at** *half past five*, **at** *midnight*
- festivals in general: **at** *New Year*, **at** *Easter*
- **at** *the weekend*, **at** *night*, **at** *the beginning*, **at** *the end*, **at** *the time*

We use *in* with:
- months, seasons, years: **in** *June*, **in** *spring*, **in** *2008*
- parts of the day: **in** *the afternoon*, **in** *the evening*
- periods of time: **in** *two weeks*, **in** *about ten minutes*

We use *on* with:
- days of the week and parts of named days: **on** *Monday*, **on** *Tuesday mornings*
- named festival days: **on** *New Year's Day*, **on** *May Day*
- dates: **on** *the 23rd of January*

We do not use *at, in* and *on* before *this, last, next* or *every*:
*The doctor doesn't see me **every** Monday, but he'll see me **next** Monday morning.*

2 Correct the mistake below.

I'll see you .... of the race.

3 Underline the correct preposition.

1 Let's meet *at /* <u>*on*</u> the 16th, then.
2 Goodnight! See you *at / in* the morning.
3 What are you doing *at / on* the weekend?
4 Our exams are *in / on* November.
5 Your appointment is *in / on* Wednesday morning.
6 I wasn't very well last year. I was working hard *at / on* the time.
7 We'll be there *at / in* about three hours.
8 I last saw Alessandra *in / on* summer 2005.

How do I use *from*, *about* and *of*?

1 Tick the correct sentence in each pair.

1 a My dad's got a radio of the 1950s.
  b My dad's got a radio from the 1950s.
2 a I'm really happy about your news.
  b I'm really happy of your news.

We use *from* to talk about:
- the place of origin: *I really want a penfriend **from** another country.*
- the distance away: *My flat is about fifteen minutes **from** the centre of town.*
- the start of a period of time: *I will be free **from** 1 pm to 6 pm.*
- the time of origin: *I have an old bicycle **from** the 1980s.*
- the start of a journey: *Take the number 10 bus **from** the bus station.*

We use *about* in the following expressions:
- *to be happy/glad/excited **about** (your visit, the weekend, your news, etc.)*
- *to read/talk/think/learn/know **about** (the job, computers, other countries, etc.)*
- *to tell someone **about** (some interesting places, your life, your trip, etc.)*

We can also say *think of.* We use the *-ing* form of verbs after prepositions:
*My sister is thinking **about** changing job.* or *My sister is thinking **of** changing job.*
*I am happy **about** seeing you at the weekend.*

We say *a book/film/programme/story **about** (animals, etc.)*
but *a picture/photo **of** (animals, etc.).*

2 Correct the mistake below.

I like reading books of food around the world.

I like reading .... around the world.

3 Complete the sentences with *from, about* or *of.*

1 I'm free ....*from*.......... midday until nearly four o'clock.
2 I like TV programmes and films .... real people.
3 Have you seen this photo .... my sister?
4 The teacher told us .... when she worked in Brazil.
5 I live three blocks .... my best friend.
6 My brother knows a lot .... computers.
7 I prefer olive oil .... Spain.
8 Are you thinking .... going to the cinema?

30 Do I need *for* in this sentence?

1 Tick the correct sentence in each pair.

1 a I don't have time to listen to music.
  b I don't have time for to listen to music.
2 a You can ask to me when you arrive.
  b You can ask for me when you arrive.

We use *for*:
- with *ask* and *wait*: *I went home. I didn't **wait for** my sister.*
- with *get/buy/sell* something + price: *I **bought** the book **for three euros**.*
- with periods of time (see Unit 12): *I've had this book **for one month**.*
- with people who get something: *I bought a present **for my brother**.*

We can use *for* + noun, or *to* + infinitive, when we say 'why':
*'Why did you go out?' 'We went out **for dinner**.'*
*We went out **to have dinner**. (= in order to have dinner.) (not **for have dinner**)*

We can say *for* + *-ing* form, or *to* + infinitive, when we talk about the use of something:
*'What do you use your mobile for?' 'I use my mobile **for texting** my friends.'*
*I use my mobile **to text** my friends. (not **for text** or **for to text**)*

We always use the *-ing* form – and not the infinitive – after *for*:
*Sorry **for being** late. (not **for be** or **for to be**)*

2 Correct the mistake below.

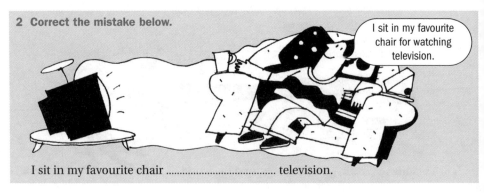

I sit in my favourite chair for watching television.

I sit in my favourite chair .... television.

3 Tick (✓) the sentences which are correct. In some pairs both sentences are correct.

1 a I'm too old for play with this. .... b I'm too old to play with this. .....✓......
2 a I went there for a check-up. .... b I went there to have a check-up. ....
3 a Thank you for helping me. .... b Thank you for help me. ....
4 a I sold it fifteen dollars. .... b I sold it for fifteen dollars. ....
5 a I got this for my sister. .... b I got this to my sister. ....
6 a I'm here for a holiday. .... b I'm here for having a holiday. ....
7 a I use it for drying my hair. .... b I use it to dry my hair. ....
8 a I sold my car to save money. .... b I sold my car for saving money. ....

Test 10

1 Underline the correct sentence ending.

1 My dentist's appointment is on *half past five / the 8th of March.*
2 We'll see each other in *the weekend / two weeks.*
3 What are you doing at *New Year / spring?*
4 The next course starts in *April / the end of the month.*
5 We don't have to go to work on *August / May Day.*
6 The party started late at *the evening / night.*
7 My friends came here in *Monday / 2005.*
8 Are the shops closed on *Saturday afternoon / the afternoon?*

2 Match the sentence endings with the beginnings.

1 Come when you like. I'll be at home	a about hospitals.
2 I'm really excited	b of leaving school.
3 We walked all the way	c about my trip to Dublin.
4 I saw a programme on TV last night	d from the bus stop.
5 That's a very nice picture	e of your parents.
6 I've been to Canada twice, so I know a lot	f from the USA.
7 I'm not sure, but I'm thinking	g about the place.
8 My teacher's name is Spanish, but he's	h from half past six.

1 ☐ 2 ☐ 3 ☐ 4 ☐ 5 ☐ 6 ☐ 7 ☐ 8 ☐

3 Add *for* to these sentences where necessary.

1 (I sold my old computer £50.) ....

2 (I'm going out a walk.) ....

3 (I use my dictionary to look up words.) ....

4 (Please wait me after school.) ....

5 (Thanks getting me this coffee.) ....

6 (We went to the café to meet our friends.) ....

7 (I lived with my grandparents five years.) ....

8 (There's a microwave heating food.) ....

4 In the box below, circle the correct word for each space, and complete the text.

Dear Pia

Thank you (1) .... your postcard and your news. The postcard arrived (2) .... three days – it was very quick! Did you have a good time in Salamanca? Where are you thinking of going (3) .... your next holiday?

This is a postcard (4) .... the Lake District in the north-west of England. We arrived two days ago and we're here (5) .... ten days. We're staying in a hotel not far (6) .... one of the lakes. I've got a guidebook, so I'm reading (7) .... all the things we can do. I'll tell you (8) .... the holiday when I write next.

Love, Judy

1 for	from	of
2 at	in	on
3 about	for	in
4 about	for	from
5 for	in	on
6 from	in	of
7 about	in	of
8 about	of	on

5 Are the sentences right or wrong? Correct those which are wrong.

1 They will pay me in the end of the month. ....

2 I'm very pleased about my new school. ....

3 I'm very sorry for to forget your birthday. ....

4 My mum has a ring of the 1920s. ....

5 I'm going shopping on next week. ....

6 Do you know very much of digital photography? ....

7 We're going on holiday at the weekend. ....

8 I went to Kate's house for talk to her. ....

Answer key

Unit 1

1 1 b
   2 a
2 computer because my old
3 2 I want a pen friend in another country, for example Australia.
   3 Before you leave England, go and visit Oxford. I love it.
   4 We saw *Syriana*, a film by George Clooney.
   5 My flatmate, who is from Russia, is very nice.
   6 I've got a sister, two brothers and a cousin. I haven't got any pets.
   7 I'm going to buy a car, so I don't need a bike.
   8 We waited ten minutes, then we decided to walk.

Unit 2

1 1 b
   2 b
2 so I decided to stay in bed
3 2 I think I will go into town and buy a shirt.
   3 I bought the book, because I liked the film.
   4 My grandparents died and I was very sad.
   5 I can play tennis, but I don't play very well.
   6 I am tired today, so I will sleep well tonight.
   7 I put the book on the shelf and (I) left the library.
   8 I hope I will see you soon.

Unit 3

1 1 b
   2 a
2 but it is
3 2 What's that girl
   3 You're not pleased *or* You aren't pleased
   4 Let's go shopping
   5 it's the eighth

   6 The book's got ... I don't like
   7 Who's speaking ... It's Jane
   8 The city's ... it's got

Test 1

1 1 sandwiches, an apple and
   2 keys, haven't I
   3 food, such as pasta and
   4 nightclub, I went home
   5 friend, who is nice, sits
   6 carrots, chop them and
   7 new, so I wear it all the time
   8 guitar, which is two years old and
2 1 a
   2 b
   3 a
   4 a
   5 b
   6 a
   7 a
   8 b
3 1 It's very hot today.
   2 We're looking forward to your visit.
   3 Maybe we'll meet our friends.
   4 I don't want my bread, so you can have it.
   5 We like our new car because it's got air conditioning.
   6 It's dark, so I need my torch.
   7 We were at home last night.
   8 I'm buying it because it costs very little.
4 1 It's half past three.
   2 My brother's job is boring.
   3 I can't remember its name.
   4 Let's have lunch.
   5 It's at the back of the book.
   6 His car's got four doors.
   7 We're not happy here.
   8 That's my friend's pen.
5 1 you'll like it
   2 my room. It's
   3 *correct*
   4 date is it
   5 dad's
   6 *correct*
   7 don't
   8 I think I will

Unit 4

1 1 b
   2 a
2 in a lovely
3 2 an interesting country
   3 a fantastic match
   4 an expensive city
   5 a lazy person
   6 a great idea
   7 an ugly block of flats
   8 a good student

Unit 5

1 1 a
   2 b
2 at the bus stop
3 2 a, a, the
   3 a, the
   4 a, a
   5 a, the
   6 the, a
   7 a, the
   8 the, the

Unit 6

1 1 a
   2 b
2 local cinema is the
3 2 the Olympic Hotel
   3 the north of Europe
   4 the Tower of London
   5 The Natural History Museum, the west of London
   6 the National Gallery
   7 The Canary Islands, the Atlantic Ocean
   8 The London Eye, the River Thames

Test 2

1 1 I watched a film on TV.
   2 I'll have some grapes and an orange.
   3 Milan is a great place.
   4 Picasso was a Spanish artist.
   5 Edinburgh has got a university.
   6 Brazil is an enormous country.
   7 I've got two brothers and a sister.
   8 Jania is an unusual name.

2 1 a a
    b the
   2 a a
    b the
   3 a The
    b A
   4 a the
    b a
   5 a the
    b a
   6 a a
    b the
   7 a the
    b a
   8 a a
    b the

3 1 a
   2 a
   3 the
   4 the
   5 a
   6 the
   7 an
   8 a

4 1 The British Museum is in Great Russell Street.
   2 Mexico is south of the United States.
   3 The London Eye is near Waterloo Station.
   4 The Statue of Liberty is in New York.
   5 Belfast is in the United Kingdom.
   6 The Andes are in the west of South America.
   7 The Dorchester is a famous hotel in London.
   8 The Canary Islands are in the Atlantic Ocean.

5 1 a book
   2 *correct*
   3 the smaller one
   4 a good cook
   5 *correct*
   6 an awful place
   7 the hall
   8 the River Thames

Unit 7

1 1 b
      2 b
2 it is fifteen years old
3 2 three years old
      3 ten-year-old
      4 is eighteen years old
      5 two-day-old
      6 twenty-four years old
      7 nine months old
      8 are eighty

Unit 8

1 1 b
      2 a
2 two o'clock in the afternoon
3 2 seven o'clock in the evening
      3 September the fourth, eighteen
         thirty-nine
      4 twenty to six (*or* five forty) in the
         morning
      5 the thirty-first of January, two
         thousand and ten
      6 eleven o'clock at night
      7 August the sixteenth, two thousand
         and two
      8 twenty-five past four (*or* four
         twenty-five) in the afternoon

Unit 9

1 1 a
      2 b
2 She needs
3 2 doesn't go (*or* does not go)
      3 come
      4 costs
      5 work
      6 tidies
      7 isn't (*or* is not)
      8 teaches

Test 3

1 1 ten-year-old
      2 thirteen-year-old
      3 one-year-old
      4 two-day-old
      5 sixteen-year-old
      6 three-month-old

      7 six-year-old
      8 fifty-year-old
2 1 b
      2 b
      3 a
      4 b
      5 a
      6 a
      7 b
      8 a
3 1 July the twentieth, nineteen sixty-
         nine *or* the twentieth of July,
         nineteen sixty-nine
      2 the twenty-fourth of August,
         eighteen seventy-five *or* August the
         twenty-fourth, eighteen seventy-five
      3 April the twenty-first, two thousand
         and one *or* the twenty-first of April,
         two thousand and one
      4 the twenty-ninth of May, nineteen
         fifty-three *or* May the twenty-ninth,
         nineteen fifty-three
      5 July the ninth, two thousand and six
         or the ninth of July, two thousand
         and six
      6 the twenty-third of April, sixteen
         sixteen *or* April the twenty-third,
         sixteen sixteen
      7 November the twenty-second,
         nineteen sixty-three *or* the twenty-
         second of November, nineteen
         sixty-three
      8 the thirty-first of December,
         nineteen ninety-nine *or* December
         the thirty-first, nineteen ninety-nine
4 1 works
      2 doesn't like
      3 finishes
      4 goes
      5 don't see
      6 stays
      7 studies
      8 doesn't want
5 1 five o'clock
      2 My parents live
      3 is thirty years old

4 doesn't like
5 *correct*
6 one year old
7 on the ninth of January
8 *correct*

Unit 10
1 1 a
  2 a
2 I bought
3 2 *correct*
  3 studied
  4 we went
  5 I took
  6 *correct*
  7 came home
  8 bought a washing machine

Unit 11
1 1 b
  2 a
2 hasn't eaten
3 2 've read *or* have read
  3 got up
  4 've hurt *or* have hurt
  5 haven't travelled *or* have not travelled
  6 didn't go *or* did not go
  7 've seen *or* have seen
  8 started

Unit 12
1 1 b
  2 a
2 I've had my guitar for
3 2 for a long time
  3 Anna has known
  4 *correct*
  5 I have had
  6 *correct*
  7 since he left
  8 We haven't played

Test 4
1 1 planned
  2 knew
  3 tried
  4 invited
  5 made
  6 put

7 arrived
8 got
2 1 I've never been *or* I have never been
  2 they've gone *or* they have gone
  3 We've eaten *or* We have eaten
  4 he's grown *or* he has grown
  5 I've left *or* I have left
  6 I haven't read *or* I have not read
  7 She's gone *or* She has gone
  8 I haven't brought *or* I have not brought
3 1 on Saturday
  2 five times
  3 until New Year's Day
  4 since last night
  5 three years ago
  6 for ten years
  7 from 2003 to 2006
  8 for three years
4 1 I waited
  2 She worked
  3 They haven't lived *or* They have not lived
  4 I've had *or* I have had
  5 We went
  6 I've known *or* I have known
  7 They got
  8 He hasn't been *or* He has not been
5 1 for ten years
  2 My friend fell
  3 has never been
  4 I haven't cut
  5 *correct*
  6 stopped
  7 My sister hasn't
  8 *correct*

Unit 13
1 1 b
  2 a
2 He's helping me
3 2 They're looking for
  3 I don't have
  4 I hope
  5 I'm selling
  6 I'm sending
  7 you're not coming
  8 We're waiting for

Unit 14

1 1 b

   2 a

2 I'm going to play tennis

3 2 they'll come

   3 I'll buy

   4 I'll see

   5 I'm going to visit

   6 you'll enjoy

   7 Shall I do

   8 it'll be

Unit 15

1 1 b

   2 a

2 Do you speak

3 2 Did you watch TV last night?

   3 Will you be there?

   4 Do you want a drink?

   5 Could you swim when you were three?

   6 Are you selling this dictionary?

   7 Have you washed your hands?

   8 Did you have lunch at home?

Test 5

1 1 'm walking *or* am walking

   2 isn't having *or* is not having

   3 lives

   4 're going *or* are going

   5 don't know *or* do not know

   6 plays

   7 's working *or* is working

   8 hope

2 1 you'll like

   2 Shall I change

   3 I won't forget

   4 We're going to see

   5 I'll help

   6 We'd love

   7 I'm going to stay

   8 you'll enjoy

3 1 Where has he gone?

   2 What has she bought?

   3 Why were you late?

   4 When did you see him?

   5 How far did she walk?

   6 What are you watching?

   7 How much (money) have you got?

   8 What time are they going out?

4 1 're feeling

   2 Did you have

   3 're coming

   4 will be

   5 'll meet

   6 would you like

   7 'll take

   8 Shall I ask

5 1 I'm going *or* I'm going to go

   2 *correct*

   3 I'm not wearing

   4 Does she like

   5 *correct*

   6 I think they'll come

   7 What are you doing

   8 I'm having

Unit 16

1 1 a

   2 b

2 There are two statues

3 2 there's

   3 they're

   4 There are

   5 it's

   6 they're

   7 it's

   8 there are

Unit 17

1 1 b

   2 a

2 some Italian food

3 2 ses – glasses

   3 ar – sugar

   4 ves – shelves

   5 ure – furniture

   6 eet – feet

   7 ion – information

   8 oks – books

Unit 18

1 1 a

   2 b

2 too much

3 2 lots of
3 much
4 a lot of
5 *both*
6 much
7 a lot of
8 *both*

Test 6
1 1 It is (*or* It's) near
2 Are there many students
3 it is (*or* it's) nice
4 There are lots of photos
5 they are (*or* they're) expensive
6 It is (*or* It's) very hot
7 There is (*or* There's) a good film
8 What date is it
2 1 books
2 fish
3 people
4 knives
5 feet
6 glasses
7 babies
8 women
3 1 There's
2 there's
3 There are
4 there's
5 There's
6 There are
7 There are
8 there's
4 1 boxes
2 men
3 time
4 teeth
5 fish
6 information
7 fruit
8 cheese
5 1 as many places
2 Too many people
3 a lot of friends *or* lots of friends
4 *correct*
5 a lot of homework
6 *correct*

7 How many countries
8 a lot of music *or* lots of music

Unit 19
1 1 a
2 a
2 I'd like to go out
3 2 We'd like
3 We didn't want
4 I don't like
5 They'd like
6 My friend wants
7 I like
8 Do you want

Unit 20
1 1 b
2 b
2 shouldn't work
3 2 *not necessary*
3 *not necessary*
4 to write
5 *not necessary*
6 to get
7 to buy
8 to do

Unit 21
1 1 b
2 a
2 I suggest going *or* I suggest we go
3 2 a
3 *both*
4 a
5 *both*
6 *both*
7 b
8 *both*

Test 7
1 1 Do you like
2 Do you want
3 Would you like
4 Does she want to go
5 Would they like to stay
6 Do they like going *or* Do they like to go
7 Would he like to play
8 Does she like watching *or* Does she like to watch

2 1 c
 2 h
 3 e
 4 a
 5 g
 6 b
 7 f
 8 d
3 1 jogging
 2 *both*
 3 running
 4 *both*
 5 using
 6 doing
 7 taking
 8 learning
4 1 to join
 2 to get
 3 to stay
 4 having
 5 playing
 6 do
 7 to be
 8 try
5 1 I'd like *or* I want
 2 to move
 3 We like
 4 *correct*
 5 I want
 6 can visit
 7 *correct*
 8 to live

Unit 22
1 1 a
 2 b
2 for another hour
3 2 other
 3 each other
 4 other
 5 others
 6 another
 7 other
 8 another

Unit 23
1 1 1 a
   2 a
2 which one
3 2 an old one
 3 the small ones
 4 easy ones
 5 the light one
 6 the old ones
 7 a slow one
 8 your short one

Unit 24
1 1 b
 2 b
2 the tallest person
3 2 hotter
 3 more interesting
 4 The best
 5 the happiest
 6 nicer
 7 the most expensive
 8 further

Test 8
1 1 a
 2 *both*
 3 a
 4 *both*
 5 *both*
 6 a
 7 a
 8 b
2 1 Paul is taller than his brother.
 2 I think politics is more interesting than sport.
 3 Midday is the hottest time of the day.
 4 Some players are worse than me.
 5 My sister's baby is the happiest of her three children.
 6 The London underground is the longest in the world.
 7 He's the most famous person in his town.
 8 I'm better at chess than my sister.

3 1 another
2 each other
3 *correct*
4 another
5 others
6 *correct*
7 each other
8 others
4 1 another one
2 The one
3 the most expensive
4 other bikes
5 cheaper
6 each other
7 worse
8 old one
5 1 I bought another (one)
2 This is the best beach
3 but not the red ones
4 *correct*
5 The longest river in the world
6 *correct*
7 Trains are faster than coaches.
8 Can I have another drink

Unit 25
1 1 a
2 a
2 the Nile, the longest river
3 2 The Pacific Ocean is the deepest ocean.
3 My new address is 761 Beach Avenue.
4 *not necessary*
5 You can meet Mr and Mrs Brown this evening.
6 The Queen's husband is called Prince Philip.
7 *not necessary*
8 The hotel is opposite Richmond Station.

Unit 26
1 1 a
2 a
2 I'm staying at
3 2 in
3 at
4 in
5 in
6 at
7 at
8 in

Unit 27
1 1 b
2 b
2 on
3 2 a
3 *both*
4 *both*
5 b
6 *both*
7 a
8 b

Test 9
1 1 a Hill
  b hill
2 a ocean
  b Ocean
3 a aunt
  b Aunt
4 a Canal
  b canal
5 a Professor
  b professor
6 a street
  b Street
7 a Princess
  b princess
8 a park
  b Park
2 1 the kitchen
2 home
3 the bottom of the page
4 hospital
5 Cambridge University
6 the sky
7 the cinema
8 the hairdresser's
3 1 on
2 by
3 –
4 in
5 by
6 on

        7 –
        8 on
4 1 in
   2 by
   3 to
   4 at
   5 on
   6 at
   7 on
   8 in
5 1 at a football match
   2 *correct*
   3 the first US president
   4 by plane *or* on a plane
   5 the largest lake
   6 Mrs Smith
   7 *correct*
   8 Dear Lola and Marcos

Unit 28
1 1 a
   2 a
2 at the end
3 2 in
   3 at
   4 in
   5 on
   6 at
   7 in
   8 in

Unit 29
1 1 b
   2 a
2 books about food
3 2 about
   3 of
   4 about
   5 from
   6 about
   7 from
   8 about *or* of

Unit 30
1 1 a
   2 b
2 to watch
3 2 *both*
   3 a

        4 b
        5 a
        6 a
        7 *both*
        8 a

Test 10
1 1 the 8th of March
   2 two weeks
   3 New Year
   4 April
   5 May Day
   6 night
   7 2005
   8 Saturday afternoon
2 1 h
   2 c
   3 d
   4 a
   5 e
   6 g
   7 b
   8 f
3 1 for £50
   2 for a walk
   3 *not necessary*
   4 for me
   5 for getting
   6 *not necessary*
   7 for five years
   8 for heating
4 1 for
   2 in
   3 for
   4 from
   5 for
   6 from
   7 about
   8 about
5 1 at the end
   2 *correct*
   3 for forgetting
   4 from the 1920s
   5 going shopping next week
   6 about digital photography
   7 *correct*
   8 to talk

Acknowledgements

The author would like to thank Thérèse Tobin for her advice and encouragement during the writing of this book.

Illustrated by Julian Mosedale

The Cambridge Learner Corpus
This book is based on information from the Cambridge Learner Corpus, a collection of over 50,000 exam papers from Cambridge ESOL. It shows real mistakes students make, and highlights which parts of English cause particular problems for learners.

The Cambridge Learner Corpus has been developed jointly with the University of Cambridge ESOL Examinations and forms part of the Cambridge International Corpus.

To find out more, visit
www.cambridge.org/elt/corpus